25 LESSONS IN HYPNOTISM

Being the Most Perfect, Complete, Easily Learned and Comprehensive Course in the World. Embracing the Science of Magnetic Healing, Telepathy, Mind Reading, Clairvoyant Hypnosis, Mesmerism, Animal Magnetism, Thought Transference, Personal Magnetism and Kindred Sciences.

British Library Cataloguing-in-Publication Data
A catalogue record for this book is available from the
British Library

CONTENTS

Hypnosis

Hypnosis has been defined as 'a special psychological state with certain physiological attributes, resembling sleep only superficially and marked by a functioning of the individual at a level of awareness other than the ordinary conscious state.' This definition captures our common understanding of hypnosis; however, research has not only revealed that hypnosis is a much more complicated thing, but it has also given rise to a number of varying definitions. One suggestion is that hypnosis is a mental state, while another links it to imaginative role-enactment.

Persons under hypnosis are said to have heightened focus and concentration with the ability to concentrate intensely on a specific thought or memory, while blocking out sources of distraction. There are many, many different methods and forms of hypnosis, but it is usually induced by a procedure known as a 'hypnotic induction', involving a series of preliminary instructions and suggestions. The hypnotic suggestions may be delivered by a hypnotist in the presence of the subject, or may be self-administered ('self-suggestion' or 'autosuggestion'). The use of these techniques for therapeutic purposes is referred to as 'hypnotherapy', while its use as a form of entertainment for an audience is known as 'stage hypnosis'.

The term 'hypnosis' comes from the Greek word *hypnos* which means sleep. However, it was first coined in 1841, by a Scottish surgeon, James Braid. He observed the occurrence of 'neuro-hypnotism' (nervous sleep), basing his practice on that developed by Franz Mesmer and his followers ('Mesmerism' or 'animal magnetism'), but differed in his theory as to how the procedure worked. Mesmer (1734–1815) believed that there was a magnetic force or 'fluid' within the universe that influenced the health of the human body. He experimented with magnets to impact this field in order to produce healing.

By around 1774, he had concluded that the same effect could be created by passing the hands in front of the subject's body, later referred to as making 'Mesmeric passes.' Later, this theory was dis-proved by many scientists, but Braid attempted to salvage part of it, replacing the supernatural theory of 'animal magnetism' with a new interpretation based upon 'common sense' laws of physiology and psychology.

Since this point, hypnosis has had a powerful and highly influential history. Sigmund Freud, the founder of psychoanalysis, studied hypnotism in Paris, and at first was an enthusiastic proponent of the method. He 'initially hypnotised patients and pressed on their foreheads to help them concentrate, while attempting to recover (supposedly) repressed memories.' He soon began to emphasise hypnotic regression and ab reaction (catharsis) as therapeutic methods. However, Freud gradually abandoned hypnotism in favour of psychoanalysis, emphasizing free association and interpretation of the unconscious. Struggling with the great expense of time that psychoanalysis required, Freud later suggested that it might be combined with hypnotic suggestion to hasten the outcome of treatment.

Hypnotism has also been used in forensics, medicine, sports, education, physical therapy, rehabilitation and relaxation. Psychiatric nurses in most medical facilities are allowed to administer hypnosis to patients in order to relieve symptoms such as anxiety, arousal, negative behaviours, uncontrollable behaviour, and improve self-esteem and confidence. This is only when they have been completely trained about their clinical side effects and while under supervision when administering it. Hypnotism has also been employed by artists for creative purposes, most notably the surrealist circle of André Breton who employed hypnosis, automatic writing and sketches for creative purposes. Hypnotic methods have been used to re-experience drug states and mystical experiences.

Self-hypnosis is popularly used to quit smoking and reduce stress, while stage hypnosis can persuade people to perform unusual public feats. Stage hypnosis is a form of entertainment, traditionally employed in a club or theatre before an audience. Due to stage hypnotists' showmanship, many people believe that hypnosis is a form of mind control. Stage hypnotists typically attempt to hypnotise the entire audience and then select individuals who are 'under' to come up on stage and perform embarrassing acts, while the audience watches. However, the effects of stage hypnosis are probably due to a combination of psychological factors, participant selection, suggestibility, physical manipulation, stagecraft, and trickery. The desire to be the centre of attention, having an excuse to violate their own fear suppressors and the pressure to please are thought to convince subjects to 'play along'.

LESSON NO. 1

I present these Lessons to the English speaking public in the belief that they will throw important light upon a subject which has too long been misunderstood and ignored.

Hypnotism is no longer one of the curiosities of Science; it is a Fact, and as such is received by the greatest minds of the age. It is creating wide-spread interest throughout our country at the present time, and well it may for it certainly is the most remarkable phenomena known to man. For years the knowledge of how to produce the hypnotic sleep has been so well guarded, that only a few have mastered the Art. Hypnotism is a scientific fact, that anyone can learn. You will be able to hypnotise people after you study these lessons, for then you will know the right methods to use to bring about this strange and wonderful control.

All may learn to hypnotise with more or less success. Some will make more rapid progress than others, on account of their devoting more time to practising, and more intense study of the different methods I herein give. Hypnotism may be defined as a condition, or induced sleep, brought about by simple methods, during which the subject is insensible to his surroundings, and yet under perfect control of the operator, who may direct his thoughts into any channel desired, and compel him to execute any command. If my instructions are followed in every detail, Hypnotism is harmless, and no harm can be done any one at any time.

I assume that you, who read these lines, intend to put the instructions I present to proper use, i. e. to make of hypnosis either an educational agent, a curative agent, or a means by which the supernormal powers of the human mind may be studied to the best advantage. I further assume that you need admonition and directions more than argument, and I therefore refrain from encumbering these lessons with theories or discussion. I give you only such reasons for certain directions as seem necessary to support the reasonableness of these directions.

I say the hypnotic condition is capable of being produced by such simple means, that it is hard for the student to believe that the methods given are the only ones needed to bring about the influence. You must disabuse your mind of this idea. You must KNOW that the chief marvels of the Hypnotic condition lie in the simple means that produces such wonderful results. You must understand that what another person does with Hypnotism, you can do also. There is nothing that you cannot do that anyone has done with this Art. You can have just as perfect control over your subjects as the greatest Hypnotist in the world. You can Hypnotize just as many at one time, in fact, you can perform any known feat ever performed by the aid of Hypnotism, just as easily and quickly as any living person.

I tell you this at the beginning, because you must have absolute confidence in yourself. You must KNOW that you will succeed. This is the first requisite to success in this Science. Before you try to Hypnotize anyone, you want to learn the first essentials for the successful induction of Hypnosis in a person who has never been Hypnotized by anyone. To do this carefully read the following pages in our book. Become familiar with these pages before going any further in this course of lessons. Do not be discouraged if your first attempts fail. Remember that the best of professional operators have difficulty in hypnotizing a person who has never been under the influence before. Commence to operate, if possible, on a person who has been hypnotized before (if there is any in your locality). You can easily induce the hypnotic sleep on an old subjet, and this fact will give you confidence and experience, for after your first success you will see just how it is. You will be amazed to find that so simple a means will bring about such wonderful results, and your enthusiasm will know no bounds. Always bear in mind that appearances count for a good deal. Never let any one know that you are a beginner. Make every one believe that you fully understand this science. After you have hypnotized several persons, the fact becomes known in your vicinity, and you will find that it is much easier to operate successfully, because every one will believe in you.

The imagination of the subject frequently has much influence with the bringing on of the hypnotic condition, and anything that will increase his confidence in your ability to hypnotize him should be taken advantage of. It is far better for you to begin your experiments on a subject that has been hypnotized before, and one who is a stranger to you, as they will have much more confidence in your ability than your friends who have never seen you perform the act of putting a subject under control.

Have confidence in yourself. Be sure that you can do what you attempt, if you expect any degree of success, or if you do not have the confidence, you must not let the fact be communicated to your subject, for if your subject realizes you do not have confidence in yourself, neither will he have confidence in you, and the experiment will plainly be a failure. The more you practice the more confidence you will have in yourself, and the more other people will have in you. Let your every word, look and action convey to the subject the impression that you will succeed. Remember that after you have hypnotized a person once, they can be hypnotized any time afterward with perfect ease.

Hypnosis follows an impression of approaching sleep made upon the mind. You cannot impress this successfully if your manner carries with it an appearance of levity. However gratifying a sense of humor may be to the possessor, a smiling operator is an unsuccessful operator. Your features should be set, firm, and stern, yet not so much so as to repel confidence. Speak low, yet firm. Be quiet in all your actions. Show no nervousness. Always keep your eyes fixed upon your subject. Be firm of will, and concentrate all your forces upon what you are doing, and you cannot fail, if you follow the methods given. Never try to use but one method at a time.

A hypnotized person is one who is possessed of no will power. He has lost the rational control over the direction of his thoughts; his mind is a perfect blank, yet it is open to receive any suggestion which may be conveyed to him by the operator, through the ordinary channels of sensation.

The method used to bring about the hypnotic conditions consists essentially in an imitation of the process of ordinary sleep, by means of verbal suggestion. Thus we actually bring sleep into existence by acting upon the imagination through action and speech. The skill of the operator consists in making the subject believe he is going to sleep; that is all. It is not necessary that he should possess any peculiarity of temperament and voice, as has been supposed. In short, everything lies in the subject and not in the operator. Impress upon your subject the belief that what you say is about to happen, will happen, and you have paved the way to success. Give your subject to understand that you are perfectly competent to hypnotize him, and his imagination will do the rest.

Assuming you are unable the get a person who has been under the influence before, I will ask you to secure a person (a stranger) who in your judgement would be easily influenced,—not one of those stubborn, over-confident know-it-all people,—but one who would be willing to obey your suggestions. The reason why some people are difficult to hypnotize is because they either consciously or unconsciously resist the operator's influence. They are not passive. Those between fifteen and twenty years of age are more easily controlled.

Having secured your subject, place him in a chair in a comfortable position, preferably with his back to the light. Before you commence to operate it will be well to observe certain conditions. First, don't let anyone talk or laugh in the room while you are operating. Disturbing noises at the first tend to prevent hypnosis. They distract the attention, and thus interfere with the mental state for hypnosis. Later when you have, as well as your subject, learned to concentrate your thoughts, noises are less disturbing. The most absolute avoidance of any sign of mistrust by those is necessary, as the least word or gesture may thwart the attempt to hypnotize. Do not allow yourself to get excited, as there is nothing whatever to get excited about. Don't be afraid that you will have any trouble in awakening your subject as that is the easiest part of it, and there is absolutely no danger of being unable to bring the subject out of the hypnotic condition if you follow strictly what these lessons teach on the subject.

LESSON NO. 2

Having observed the above precautions, you may now turn your attention to hypnotizing your subject. You have put him into a comfortable chair, and make sure that he is comfortable. Shift him about until he is resting easily, and say that he is resting. You do this for effect. Everything in this work depends upon the effect you produce upon the subject's mind. You are not, while engaged in this work, a man of original thoughts; you are simply an actor, weighing tone and gesture, testing the effect of a glance, a sentence, a frown, a compression of the lips, a persuasive unbending; testing these things, weighing them, withdrawing them according to results, even as the regular physician tries and withdraws his material remedies according to results.

Before beginning your work as the hypnotizer (no matter which method you use), your subject is to look at whatever you may request him to, and say to him that very soon he will become drowsy, then more and more drowsy, until he will be compelled to close his eyes and sleep. Be sure to tell him that he will notice nothing unusual about the drowsiness; tell him that it will be just as pleasant as the approach to natural sleep that he has ever experienced. Let him not expect anything unnatural to occur, for such will distract his attention and make him feel excited and less passive than he should be. Let him understand that it is for his good to be hypnotized if he is sick, or to help him cure a bad habit. Tell him that you will not make him appear ridiculous, and that you will only keep him asleep for a few minutes. Tell him to look earnestly at whatever you direct, and never under any circumstances to look away from it; no matter who comes into the room or around him he is going to gaze straight at the object and no other.

METHOD No. 1.—Take any bright object (I generally use my watch), between the thumb and fore and middle fingers of the right hand. Be sure that the light falls in the object in your hand. Hold it from eight to twelve inches from the eyes, at about ten inches above the head so as to produce the greatest possible strain upon the eyelids, and enable the subject to maintain a fixed steady stare at the object. The subject's eyes must be fixed steadily on the bright object, and his mind riveted upon the idea of the one object. When you notice the first change in your subject's face and eyes say such words as these: "Keep right on looking at it, directly you will be drowsy. You are sleepy. Your eyelids are heavy. You are asleep." Let your voice grow lower, lower, till just above a whisper. Pause a moment or two. Give him time. Never hurry. You will fail if you try to hurry too much at first. He will think it more natural if you give him a moment to get sleepy. Let him only listen. As soon as the eyelids really grow heavy, say: "Your eyes are almost closed now," making your words long drawn out and spoken in a tone which will not arouse him, but will, instead, indicate that you are yourself sleepy—and almost gone. Continue as follows: "Directly your eyes will have to close—you just cannot keep awake—see they are closing—now they are almost ready to close—now they will close and you will sleep. Close them." Pause a moment, then say: "Sleep." Give the command to sleep in a quiet, yet firm and masterful way, in a low tone.

You will see that the eyelids may quiver for a few seconds, sometimes for a minute, but very soon the subject will settle back in his chair, frequently with a sigh, and the eyes will become quiet, and his limbs show perfect relaxation. Let him remain so for some minutes, saying nothing to him at all. When you are ready to operate, it is well for you as a beginner, especially if you have a new subject, to constantly make suggestions. For instance, you say: "Nothing will wake you, nothing can hurt you. You can open your eyes, but you will stay asleep. Now I am about to raise your arm, but you won't wake up. Nothing will wake you." Rub the arm a few times and say: "Now you can't take it down—see, you can't. You are sound asleep, and you will do everything I tell you to do, but you will not wake up—you can't wake up till I tell you."

The arm will remain in the position in which it is placed, and if you tell him that no person can take it down or bend it, you will find it true that no one can. I always begin operations in this way, placing both arms in an uplifted position, with both legs outstretched in the same manner. When you are ready to take them down rub them gently but firmly (rubbing from the body, and always raising the hands when reaching the extremities) and say: "Now you can take them down—see, you can—you will do all I tell you. You will have to do so. No one can wake you except myself." Speak to your subject just as though he were awake and in full possession of his senses. Although fast asleep to every one else, he is keenly awake to you. He went to sleep with his mind absorbed with the idea that you alone could control him, and this is the reason why no one else can make any impression on him. This connection between the subject and operator is called rapport, which is a state of sleep in which the attention of the subject is fixed exclusively upon the Hypnotist, so that the idea of him is constantly present in the subject's memory. It is possible, however, to put your subject en-rapport with any other person by simply suggesting to him to he is to obey the requests or demands of that person until further notice.

METHOD No. 2.—The subject reclines on a couch or easy chair, and you stand beside him. Hold the first two fingers of your right hand at a distance of about twelve inches from his eyes, at such an angle that his gaze shall be directed upwards in a strained manner. Direct him to look steadily at the tips of those fingers, and to make his mind as nearly blank as possible. After he has stared fixedly for about half a minute his expression will undergo a change—a far away look coming into his face. His pupils will contract and dilate several times, and his eyelids will twitch spasmodically. These signs indicate a commencement of the desired hypnotization. If the eyes do not close of themselves, shut them gently with your left hand, and say: "You are becoming sleepy; your eyes are very heavy; they are getting more and more heavy; my fingers seem quite indistinct to you (this when the pupils are observed to dilate or contract); a numbness is stealing over your limbs; you will be fast asleep in a few minutes; now sleep."

This is a good method to use with children, and if they are hypnotized for any special reason hold their right hand with your left while talking to them.

METHOD No. 3.—Seat your subject if convenient in an ordinary chair (not an arm or rocking chair), with both feet flat upon the floor. Place his hands on his thighs with the palms down, the fingers pointed towards the knees. Then, standing three or four feet in front of him, request him to relax as much as possible, mentally and physically. Then say to him: "Look at one of my eyes," and draw his attention with the index finger of your right hand to the eye you wish him to look at. Lower your hand immediately to your side, and gaze directly and steadily into one of your subject's eyes until his pupil begins to dilate. This will require from five to ten seconds. Then repeat slowly the following: "Close your eyes gently—arch your eye-brows. Now you will find it hard to open your eyes. Try—try—try! All right, you may open them." Relax all tension in yourself when you say "All right." You must, of course, feel confident that you can hold his eyes closed for a few seconds. Your manner and tone should be such as to convince him that you can do so. As soon as you see that you have produced an impression at once release your subject for a moment. This will prevent his forming adverse auto-suggestions which might destroy the slight impressions already made. After a moment's rest, repeat the operation, saying again: "Look at one of my eyes. Close your eyes gently," and so on, just as before. From the moment you commence keep up a stream of oral suggestions, and repeat the above over and over again until you are quite sure your subject is under your influence.

LESSON NO. 3

Supposing sleep to be induced, the next and very important question is how to awaken the subject. With the most sensitive persons this is a very easy process, for merely blowing or fanning over the head and face with a few transverse passes will at once dispel the sleep. Should, however, the subject experience a difficulty in opening his eyes, then with the tips of the thumbs the operator should rub briskly from the root of the nose outwards toward the temples, and finish by blowing or fanning, take special care before leaving the subject that—judging from the expression of the eyes and face—he has evidently returned to his normal condition. As a rule the subject should not be left until the operator is perfectly certain that he is wide awake. This method of awaking is used by the most noted hypnotists in the world.

Many subjects can be awakened by the simple command, "Awake," "All right," "Wake up." At the same time snapping your thumb and finger close to their faces. In other cases tell your subject to count ten, and that when he gets to nine he will wake up. But in some cases of deep hypnosis these methods all fail, even after repeated trials, what then shall you do? I must say the only danger of hypnotism is in the inability to awaken the subject from the sleep. The danger is not caused by the hypnotic sleep, but by the fear that the operator shows, which make a doubt enter the mind of the subject, who then loses confidence in you, and he also doubts if you can control the POWER you have thrown over him. Never shake your subject, or allow yourself to feel or exhibit any alarm. If your subject does, not awaken easily, leave him alone quietly for a few minutes. Do not speak or appear to notice him. Then after three or four minutes, turn to him suddenly, and say in a stern voice: "I command you to awaken." This generally succeeds. If it does not, after repeating the command several times, making the command more positive each time, you can rest assured that he is not under your control in regard to the walking process. Should none of the methods succeed in awaking him, it is a scientific fact that he is under his own control. Now there are two ways of doing. First: Put him into a comfortable position and he will go into natural sleep, and after some time awaken all right. Second (And to consider this the better way): Ask the subject what you must do to awaken him. Sometimes he will say to let him sleep, one, two, three or more hours, and he will awake. In such a case say to your subject, "All right, at exactly the time specified you will awaken. Remember, you must awake," designating some certain hour if possible, "and then you will awake bright and refreshed." Set or lay him in any easy position, and do not bother him until the time arrives set for him to wake up.

Often he will wake without your doing or saying anything, but if he does not, go to him and say: "All right, your time is up, wake at once." Slap your hands together close to his head while you are speaking, and he will instantly awake. In another case he will tell you something to do and he will then wake up, such as pull one of his fingers one or more times, or to pinch him, or to slap him, or some other seemingly foolish thing, but in every case do exactly as he tells you, no matter how absurd it may seem to you, and you will never have any trouble in awaking him. Be sure to learn thoroughly how to awaken your subjects by these methods before you put any one to sleep, because if you don't you may have some trouble in your experiments. Always have these lessons with you if you do not thoroughly remember how to awaken your subjects, so you can turn to these rules and follow them out explicitly.

LESSON NO. 4

METHOD No. 4.—Hypnotic Sleep Brought About by Suggestion.—Select for your patient a man who believes in you, one who has some bodily ill that he feels sure you can relieve, if not cure. Yet he has hopes that you win eventually entirely cure him. Place the patient in a chair, follow directions given in Method No. 2. Your patient is obedient because he believes in you. He is passive of his own accord. You have his co-operation, he wants to be hypnotized. You stand directly before him, with clasped hands, falling at arm's length, and sinking your voice to a soothing montone, say: "You are resting quietly. Mr.——, and you will make no special effort to attend to anything I say, because effort of any kind will have the effect of rousing you from the dreamy condition of content and drowsiness that is approaching, you will keep your eyes fixed on mine while I speak, but as your head becomes cool, and the blood leaves the brain, your eyes will have a tendency to close, and drowsiness, even a lethargy, will follow. Your thoughts will come slower. You are not anxious about anything. You are simply passing into a state of natural sleep. Your breathing is slower, deeper, quieter. Your heart beats more slowly, the whole system is soothed and rested, and you are becoming' oblivious to your surroundings. Your mental condition is one of quiet and rest, and you are inducing sleep in yourself by this process. Your eyes are becoming heavy, drowsiness is upon you, following as it naturally must upon your quiet state of physical and mental relaxation. Your eyes are becoming heavy, heavier, drowsy and quiet, don't resist the influence of approaching sleep, don't think, don't reason, don't argue with yourself, don't worry about anything. Let me do the work, just be content to rest. Now you go a little further—a little drowsier. Your arms and legs are heavy. Your eyes are closing, closing, let them close now tightly, tightly closed, now quiet and still, and you are going sound asleep." Lay your fingers lightly on his eyelids for a few moments, repeating: "Sleep quietly, no nervousness, outside noises will not trouble you, nothing can disturb you, quiet and comfortable." Now make light passes, barely touching his clothes, slowly from his head to his feet, repeating: "Quiet and comfortable, going soundly away to sleep," etc. Keep this up for five minutes, and here I may pause a moment to point out how vitally necessary to success is that condidtion of mental content which you have taken so much trouble to induce. Unless your patient were content he would now be anxiously waiting for what you were to do next, he would be arguing with himself that he was not asleep, was not sleepy, did not feel sleepy, and he would work himself up into a fine state of excitement and antagonism. But you have impressed upon him that he is thoroughly satisfied with you and with himself, and he accordingly has sufficient confidence in you to let things happen as they will. You must continue as above till quite sure that he is well under your control, then you want to treat him by suggestion. This method is one that in the hands of doctors must meet with splendid results. Later we describe a case being treated by suggestions. By studying it carefully you will see just what to say and what to do. Such treatment is called Suggestive Therapeutics. Mind Healing is done in the same way, and is the same thing. The man wants to be cured. He has faith in you. You assure him that you will do for him all you can. He believes, and with the aid of hypnotism and his faith the cure is made by God, who uses you as His instrument. That is all this wonderful power possesses.

METHOD No. 5.—Hypnotizing with passes is an excellent method for producing the phenomena. Follow directions of Method No. 1—in placing, etc. You stand opposite your subject, place your hand with extended fingers over his head, and make passes slowly down to his extremities, as near the face and body as possible without touching the subject, taking care at the end of each pass to close your hands until you return to his head, when you should again extend your fingers and proceed as before. It is also usual, after making several of the passes, to point the fingers close to the subject's eyes, which procedure in many cases has more effect than passes. You want to speak to the subject in the same low tone, and much in the same manner as in Method No. 4. This simple process should be continued for about twenty minutes at the first trial, and may be expected to produce more or less effect according to the susceptibility of the subject. Should you perceive no signs of approaching sleep you should persevere with the passes until the eyes close, and should you then observe a quivering of the eyelids, you may be pretty certain that your effort will be successful. Many experienced hypnotists have come to the conclusion that the will plays an important part in the production of the sleep and in relief of pain. Whether this be the case or not, it is recommended that you should concentrate your energies, and earnestly will or wish that your subject should derive benefit from your exertions. Some very susceptible subjects in the course of ten minutes or even less time, will suddenly fall back apparently insensible, in which case the following tests will prove whether or not the real hypnotic coma has been produced. Raise the subject's hand, and should it fall immediately as a dead weight it is a good sign, then raise the eyelids and should the eye-ball be observed to be upwards and wandering in its orbit, there can be little doubt of your success. In some cases the eye-ball will be found in its natural position but with the pupil much dilated, no contraction taking place on the approach of a lighted candle. Even at this early stage the subject may bear the prick of a pin on the back of his hand without betraying any symptom of pain. Sometimes the breathing or placing the hand on the forehead will deepen the sleep, but the beginner should, as a rule, avoid concentrating the hypnotic force on the head or region of the heart, and confine himself as much as possible to the passes, long, slow passes from the head to the feet. Should the before-described signs of hypnotic coma not declare themselves at the end of twenty or thirty minutes you should ask the subject whether he felt any peculiar sensation during the process, and, if so, whether they were apparent during the passes or when the fingers were pointed to the eyes. By these inquiries you will soon learn the best method of hypnotizing applicable to each particular subject and you should not be disheartened if you do not succeed in producing marked effects at the first, or even many unsuccessful trials. Supposing sleep to be induced, it is the next and very important question to awaken your subject. With this method a few transverse passes (throwing off with both hands, right and left), will at once dispel the sleep. If not, read Lesson No. 3, which will tell you what to do. The use of passes is very essential in many cases where the subject is a sufferer of great pain.

LESSON NO. 5

POST-HYPNOTIC SUGGESTIONS.—One of the most wonderful and puzzling feats of hypnotism is what is called Post-Hypnotic Suggestion. In this test suggestions are made to the subject when he is asleep. He is then awakened, and in his natural waking state he carries the suggestions out not knowing from whence he received the command. In giving an evening's entertainment these tests under posthypnotic suggestion will prove the most mystifying, as you will see further on in these lessons. You will will more fully understand the wonder of this strange power after you study later pages. From them you will see how easy it is to wield this influence which, if not understood, seems impossible.

HYPNOTIZING BY TELEPHONE.—If a telephone is convenient, as a matter of scientific experiment you might hypnotize some one by this means. This is a most startling feat, and never fails to astonish every one present. Of course, it is understood by you that you must have hypnotized your subject before, and have suggested to him while in the hypnotic sleep that should you send him a telephone message he will instantly he hypnotized without your actual bodily presence. It is always well to inform the subject that when he is hypnotized by telephone that he will awaken voluntarily at the end of ten or twenty minutes, just as you may wish. Only tell him one time to awaken. It is unlikely that you will have occasion to use this method to any great extent, but it will create a great deal of astonishment among your friends if you should give your subjects a posthypnotic suggestion of this character, then send him to another town and hypnotize him by telephone or telegraph. Either one will answer, but it must be the one suggested to him when hypnotized. Always remember that you can make but one suggestion to your subject at a time. Then, too, if you use this method of hypnotizing at a distance, it will create a very good impression in your vicinity in regard to your ability as a hypnotic operator. You can hypnotize in the same way by telling your subject that when he receives a letter from you that he must go at once into the hypnotic state.

LESSON NO. 6

MESMERISM.—Place your patient in an easy chair. Seat yourself in front of him, with the patient's knees between your own, and laying hold of both his hands with your thumbs to each other. Concentrate your attention upon your patient, and ask him to look steadily at you. Hold his hands till there is an equilibrium of heat established. Then make passes slowly from the forehead to the pit of the stomach, and from the crown of the head down both sides of the neck, and along both arms to the fingers. The eyes of the subject show if you are making progress, as they will begin to follow your hands, and a peculiar tremor of the lids or a long heavy wink is observed. The eyes at last close, but the eyelashes generally continue to quiver, as if from an instinctive attempt to open them. This the patient cannot now do, even though he may still retain his general sensibility. The process being continued at last brings on the mesmeric coma, which, being tested, you can perform. One of the easiest tests is—if you swallow, the patient does likewise. You pinch your own arm, the subject jumps as if it were his arm that had been pinched. Prick your hand and the subject feels it. Many operators find this method of mesmerism one of the very best when amusement is the object wished to be obtained. To awaken your patient from this influence make rapid reverse passes, bringing your hands from the feet to the head, open your hands every time you bring them near the head, making the same movement as if you were throwing something away. Fanning the face will also awaken him.

MESMERISM AND HYPNOTISM are so closely united that they can be well called the twin brothers of this age. Brothers so closely united that the scientific world does not all agree about where to draw the dividing line between them. I shall not try to do so, but after you have carefully learned these lessons and read my book, you can judge for yourself which you can handle with the best results. Whatever method you choose will be the right one for you. To beginners it is a good plan to learn to be successful with the method that seems the most easy to you. Then master another one, and it will not be long till you are at home with them all. If you select Method No. 1, and do not own a watch, you can use a finger ring with a stone in it, or a gold pencil, or a teaspoon, or if you want something that people will not know what it is you can cover a round piece of wood with gilt foil or gold leaf. You can get it from any painter. Fasten same on a short stick or on the end of a pencil. A round piece of pine wood, a little larger than an ordinary marble and that up—any of the above will bring the hypnotic sleep. The way to make a magic mirror also is shown here.

LESSON NO. 7

MAGNETIC HEALING holds an important place in science today, and many wonderful cures are laid at its doors. The following is the mode to bring about the wonders that I know you are anxious to perform. Mesmerize your patient as Method given in last lesson, or as Method No. 2. When your patient is magnetized, he is fully under your control, and you must be careful not to say or do anything to alarm your patient, or he will awaken suddenly, and the harm is great. You have for a patient a man who has been a great sufferer from rheumatic pains. You have succeeded in inducing sleep. He is lying on a sofa. The part most affected is his legs. You make several passes from his waist down to his feet. Open your hands when you reach the feet, throw out the fingers their full length. Close them quickly, and begin again. Make these passes several seconds, then begin at the head and bring your hands to the feet; do this several seconds, opening your hands each time. Do this till you are sure your patient is very sound asleep. Then begin with the right arm. Rub it from the armpit to the ends of the fingers. Rub it well from underneath as well as on top. Rub with a firm, gentle pressure, opening your hands each time you reach the fingers. Manipulate the arm till the hand is warm, and, if possible, moist. Then lay it down gently and cover up. Do the same to the left arm. Then the right side and back; then the left side and chest. Then the right limb, and last, the left limb, opening the hands at the end of each pass. Let the longest and firmest rubbing be on the legs where the pain is the most intense. The sore places must be rubbed and kneaded gently. It is well to put a little vaseline on the hands, as they will rub smoother and be pleasanter to the patient if you rub next the skin. Although many operators work outside the clothes. Let the manipulations of the body last at least thirty to forty minutes. After all the body has been thoroughly heated, rub the head, neck and face. When you begin treating the head begin to talk to your patient in a low, slow tone, as follows: "You feel very much better now. You will keep getting better till all the pain has gone, and you are well. You will not have any such pain again. You are well. You are perfectly well and comfortable. Your arms and legs and your whole body is free from pain." Stop rubbing his head and take his hands in yours. Concentrate all your will and still hold his hands firmly, continue, "The pain has gone away. You can move as well as you ever did in your life. You will have no more—no more pain. Remember—no more pain." Speak in a long, drawn-out, low voice. After a few moments, in which all is quiet, awaken him. And he will tell you how much better he is. If possible, treat him every day for a week, and you will have him entirely cured.

ANIMAL MAGNETISM, means animal electricity, and

the force or power often passes through your hands, as you hold the hand of a person less strong than yourself. That is why manipulation of the body means so much to the patient when the operator is strong, healthy, and fully understands his power, and how to massage the body as it should be done. We all to a greater or less extent exert our influence over others, and that perhaps is the reason why this magnetism is so firmly believed in, and is said to be natural to all, but highly developed in a few. This power pervades the universe, but is most active in the human, nervous organization, and enables any man charged with this force to exert a wonderful influence over others. To use this means of affecting another, the method is much like the one given above. Make your patient look steadily at your eyes. You command him mentally to become quiet. In a few minutes he will feel a creeping sensation stealing over his body, and he will fall into a sleep. You then rub thoroughly whatever part of the body is in pain. If you have a patient who objects to being put to sleep, and does not believe in hypnotism of any sort, it is a good plan to say nothing to him about going to sleep. Put him into a comfortable position, and begin to treat him by rubbing the body. Concentrate your mind on him, and be determined that he shall sleep, and long before you are through treating him he will be in a mesmeric sleep, then suggest to him, "that the treatment will make him well." This is one way of using animal magnetism.

LESSON NO. 8

HOW TO CURE BAD HABITS. In many homes this is the most important part of hypnotism. Ask your subject to assume a comfortable position on a lounge, or in an easy chair. Then lead her into an easy, soothing conversation in which you do the talking. Giving no chance for more than a yes or no from her. Manage in a way determined by the circumstances of the case to concentrate her gaze on something you hold in your hand, the usual distance from her face and eyes. See Method No. 2 for further directions. A ring with an odd stone in it is a good subject to hold, and about it you can weave a romance that will hold the mind and imagination. If your subject is young, tell her that the stone in the ring is very rare, and that it is known as the "Sleepy-stone." Tell her it has never failed to induce slumber, and that the stone is only found in the most remote part of India. Insist that she listen to you, and only thinks of the strange, wonderful slumber that it gives. If she knows why she is being hypnotized, you can add, the charm of this slumber never leaves the sleeper, and that it has so strange a power that its help is always brought into action when you are determined to give relief, and break up the habit that is so harmful. This appeal to the imagination is of very great help when the subject is a child or young person.

To older persons you Cannot be so romantic. In all cases you must use your best judgment.

After the subject has gazed at the ring for a few seconds or minutes, you will see the same change in her face before described. When the change in her expression begins lower your voice, saying the words slower, as following: "Slumber now, gently, quietly, s-l-u-m-b-e-r." Pause a second. "Sleep, s-l-e-e-p, s-l-u-m-b-e-r," pause and drawl out the words long—but be sure you speak clearly, yet low. Now move your hand if her eyes are closed. If they are not, with your unoccupied hand close her eyelids very, very gently. Rub them lightly, downward, saying all the while, "Slumber, keep your eyes closed, sleep peacefully." Move your hand from her eyes, and put away the ring. With both hands gently make passes over her face—from the forehead downward. Do not touch her face. Have your hands about two inches from her. Do this Several times, till you know she sleeps soundly. Do not speak while you are doing this. To cure bad habits of any kind the hypnosis must be deep as possible. While she is under this influence you want to speak firmly, yet gently. You must talk to her in a manner that would gain her confidence. You want to gain her faith, to make her know and believe that you are only anxious for her good. If you want to cure her of nail-biting, say, "You have a very beautiful hand, but do you know that you are trying to spoil it by biting your nails. Do you know that the beauty and shapeliness of your fingers lie in their having well kept and handsome nails, and if you continue biting them your really beautiful hand will be spoiled? You don't want to do that, do you? You want to always have a handsome hand. I know you do, so promise me not to bite your nails—promise me—not to bite your nails—again—promise—promise promise me—not to bite your nails again—promise me to try to keep your beautiful hands. Don't bite your nails any more." From the first promise repeat over and over if need be, till her word is given.

If your subject is a bad boy, put him to sleep the same as above. Be sure to get him as soundly and as deeply hypnotizd as you can before you begin to operate on him. Then talk to him in a friendly way, just as you would have liked a man to talk to you when you were a boy. Let your voice be gentle, and the tone the same as if you were trying to soothe a fretful baby. Very much of your success depends on your voice in these bad habit cases. Talk to him in a friendly way till the cross or angry look leaves his face. Tell him that you are his friend, and that you know just how hard it is to mind and please grown up people. Tell him that when you were a boy that you felt just as you know he feels, and that is why you are going to give him your advice because you know it will help him to do the very things that you know he wants to do. After a little he will smile, and you have gained a point. When he smiles he is ready for your suggestion. Keep your voice low, and take one or both of his hands in yours, and be sure to keep your eyes on his face, your entire will concentrated on him. "Sleep deeply—sleep deeply"—repeat till you are sure he is well under your influence. Then begin in earnest, saying, "You a bad boy? No! No! You are a bright, manly boy. You are always going to be good now. Sleep on, and dream of being good. You are a good boy. You will never strike your sister again. You will never lie. No! No! You are a good boy. You will play with the other children. You will not fight the other boys—because sunshine is in your heart, and sunshine is in your mind. You are a good, bright, loving boy. You love your mother. You love your mother, and you will always mind her—because—you—love—your—mother. Sleep—my good—my obedient boy—my—good—boy. Sleep—you—always—mind—your—mother. You—love—to—obey. My good boy, my bright boy, my happy boy, my good boy." Rub his forehead gently, and call him "your good boy" over and over till you have it firmly fixed in his mind that he is good. Say, "You are a good boy. You are a happy boy, and you can never be anything but good. Every one loves you, you are so good. You good boy."

Let good boy be the last thing you say to him before you wake him. Try also to impress upon his parents that they must do their part after he is awakened, and that they must help him by being very, very careful not to find fault with him or call him bad. They must not nag him, but help him, or all the good you have done they can and will destroy. Often failure is caused by the people who are around the child between the times of the first two or three treatments.

In putting your patients into the hypnotic sleep for curing any habit, you can use any method that you are the most successful with, only be sure that the sleep is deep. It is always a good plan to get the promise if you can. From the above you can easily see that with hypnotism and the aid of post-hypnotic suggestion any and all bad habits can be broken, if you only insist, and give enough treatments.

LESSON NO. 9

To induce clairvoyant hypnosis is perhaps one of the most difficult stages to bring about in the ordinary subject. Still it can be done, and when this stage is reached successfully it is very wonderful, and well worth the trouble it may be to the operator.

To induce this hypnotic sleep, Method No. 6 is the best. By many this is known as the Mental Method. Tell your subject to close his eyes. Tell him that his mind is a perfect blank. Command him to think of nothing. Remain very passive and quiet for a few seconds. Then speak in a low voice, "You cannot open your eyes." If he does not open them, remain quiet again. Always keep your eyes firmly fixed upon him. Speak again, repeating, "You cannot open your eyes, but you can see the place I send you to. Look about you. You cannot open your eyes." Put your hand upon his wrist, with your fingers over his pulse. Keep your eyes upon him. Say in a slow, low voice, "Now describe what you see. Look—closely—look—what do you see?" All the while you must think of the place he is to see. It makes no difference whether you have ever been there or not, the thought helps him. If the subject is well under your influence, he will accurately describe the place you are thinking of, even if hundreds of miles away, and places that neither one of you have ever seen. If you have a very sensitive subject you may be able to have him hear conversations carried on in other rooms, or even when the parties are far away, as well as describe what people are doing. For easier tests you can have some one tell you where to send the subject (out of his hearing), and by holding his hand he will do or go wherever or whatever you think about.

THOUGHT TRANSFERENCE OR TELEPATHY is another wonderful stage. After you have your subject hypnotized, which you may induce by any of the methods you wish, you can have him do anything you think about. Hold his hand, and repeat mentally any verse you wish, and the subject will repeat it out loud. Order him to do anything mentally and he will do it. You act as one person, your mind and the subject's body being as one person. You do the thinking, he does the act. There are many wonderful feats recorded under this wonderful science. No one can explain them or tell where they will lead to.

LESSON NO. 10

Somnambulism is the stage in which much can be done. Many subjects are thrown into this stage the very first time they are hypnotized. Others will not be thrown into this stage until it is suggested to them. Somnambulism means deep sleep, in which the subject will carry out any suggestions made by the operator. You have been taught to hypnotize by verbal suggestion. I now will teach you how to induce passive somnambulism in the sleeper. Before your patient will pass easily into somnambulism he must sleep very, very soundly. It is always better, therefore, not to attempt to induce this condition until he has became accustomed to being hypnotized. I never try to induce somnambulism till the patient has at least been asleep three times. It is quite possible that your patient may be asleep when you do not know it, but there is one test by which you may know certainly that he does sleep. Watch the eyelids, and if you see the ball of the eye rolling rhythmically and evenly from side to side like the movement of a pendulum, he is asleep and dreaming. He may be asleep when the eyeball is still, but if you notice this slow, rhythmical movement, sleep is assured.

A condition of passive somnambulism is one in which the

patient realizes the suggestions of the operator to such a degree that the suggestion or word pictures take the form of vivid dreams. These suggested dreams differ from the ordinary kind in that they are amenable to suggestion from without at any moment. They can be altered, shattered, reconstructed at the pleasure of the operator. Induced sleep is easily turned into somnambulism because the patient is expecting the voice of the operator. The patient passes into the state of somnambulism in the first place only because he is quite content to listen to the operator's voice and take suggestions.

It is not necessary to more than hint to you how readily the wife might benefit the husband, or the husband the wife. Once understood and it is only necessary for the sleeper to become accustomed to the presence of another party to change natural sleep into induced sleep, and you understand how easily parent, wife or husband could enter into relationship with the sleeper, and talk to without waking the latter. Thus natural sleep may be turned into induced or hypnotic sleep. It is simply a question of reaching the sleeper just so far as to get his attention, but not so far as to wake him. If you have not the sleeper's attention, then your sleeper is in a natural sleep. If you have his attention, then he is in a state identical with induced sleep. Therefore, the differentiating point between the natural sleep and the induced sleep is—the attention of the sleeper. This and nothing more.

I begin to induce somnambulism as follows: When the

patient is, as I think, asleep, I make slow passes over the body, scarcely touching the clothing, repeating in a low voice the following: "Quiet and comfortable; going further and further and further away to sleep; nothing disturbs you; you are quiet and still."

Continue the passes for five minutes, repeating always, very quietly, "Further and further away to sleep." Then say, still very quietly—your voice must carry no shock with it, because a shock at this stage would bring back consciousness of environment which is wakefulness—"Further and further away. Your mind goes back now more and more vividly to a scene, a landscape, which gave you once great pleasure. It is some place you visited or lived in long ago. There are hills, trees and water, all there, clear and distinct before you. You are going back in spirit place, leaving here, going back. You are not here. You will not come back here till I wake you. You will live in that scene. You will go through the same experiences, happy experiences, which you went through there before, point for point, word for word. You will meet the same people, hear the same words, feel as well and as strong as you did then. This will not be a dream to you, it will be reality. You will move in this scene among those people. Everything will be vivid and real to you. Go further and further away, back to that scene." Sit still for fifteen minutes, and in nine cases out of ten, your patient will dream the very thing suggested. Yet, on waking, there will be the distinct consciousness of having sleep, and he will remember the dream or not, just as you suggest. If the sleep is light, the dream is likely to be recalled by the sleeper, unless you order him to forget it. But in cases where the somnambulism is very deep—where the patient is so wrapped in his vision that he cannot be drawn into conversation during its continuance, without disturbing the thread, there is seldom any memory on waking. In perfect somnambulism you have perfect amnesia. Before giving the suggestion to awake, I usually give such therapeutic suggestions as the case calls for, and then add that when he wakes he will be refreshed. Then I tell him that he will awake in five minutes, and I leave him alone. At the expiration of the time I go back and, as a rule, he is awake—himself—again.

LESSON NO. 11

METHOD NO. 7.—This is my Special Method, when your subject is a nervous woman. Make your patient comfortable on a sofa. Tell her to relax her muscles, and see that she does so. Then attend to her breathing, see that she breathes slowly and evenly—with regularity, not in spasms or jerks—from the abdomen. If necessary spend half an hour in teaching her how. Draw your chair up beside her, and lay your hand lightly over the pit of her stomach. Your chair should be so placed that you can maintain this attitude without inconvenience to yourself. Always remember you gain nothing by making the work hard. Your patient is comfortable and expectant. She is breathing quietly. The room is shaded from all glare. Begin your suggestions thus: "Keep your eyes upon mine. Do exactly as I bid, and you will go to sleep. I shall not give you any suggestions during your treatment or afterward. You are quiet, and they are not necessary. After your sleep you will feel much better. Your pain will be less—will be gone. Your nerves will be quiet and stronger. Now I shall count aloud. When I count 'one,' close your eyes; when I count 'two,' open them; 'three,' close them; 'four,' open them, and so on. Outside noises will not trouble you; nothing will distract you. You are going to sleep. Ready. 'One'." Count up to twenty, then go back to one again, and repeat as often as necessary. The art of using this method successfully consists in lengthening the intervals between counts.

TO CURE INSOMNIA.—Hypnotize your patient by any method you please, and use the post-hypnotic suggestion as follows: "You are asleep now, and remember you are to go to sleep at ten o'clock—at ten oclock—every night till I forbid it—at—ten—o'clock—every—night—till—I—forbid—you—to. Remember, at ten o'clock. And you are to sleep—to sleep—I say, till six in the morning. You are to sleep from ten o'clock at night till six in the morning—every—night—till—I—forbid—it. Remember." You want to repeat it over and over, and get a promise from your patient if you can. If you do not cure him in the first treatment, try again, as I have never known it to fail.

METHOD NO. 7 is good to use for all nervous twitching. It is done by the post-hypnotic suggestion. It is also a good plan to rub the part affected while talking to your subject. Tell your subject always that when she wakens the nervousness will be gone. Stammering can be cured in the same way. Some have succeeded by following directions given in Lesson No. 9.

To hypnotize a sick person without their knowledge is often a very great help, such sleep can be induced by will power. The patient expects you, her doctor, to relieve her, and her confidence in you is what will give you the control that otherwise would be difficult to obtain. Stand at the head of the bed, in such a position that the patient's eyes will be strained to look at you. Take her hand in yours. Gently rub her head, and talk in a low, soothing manner, as—"You are suffering, I know, but will soon be better. I know you will, because I shall stay here until you sleep. Sleep is what you need and must have." Keep your right fingers on her wrist, and gently bring the fingers of your left hand down over her eyes, closing the eyelids. "You will be better when you wake. Yes—almost well. Sleep—is—what—you—need. Sleep—is—coming. Sleep—now—sleep." After a few minutes of such work your patient will sleep, and she will wake herself at any hour you suggest, and will be much refreshed and better.

LESSON NO. 12

Many children suffer from illusions or hallucinations, which can be cured by their mother hypnotizing them and ordering such whims away. Many claim that children can not be hypnotized; such is true in some cases, and might be in nearly all if the operator be a stranger, but when the mother tries to hypnotize her child she nearly always succeeds. The best instructions to follow are given in Lesson No. 8. If they shall fail, then perhaps the child is too young to be hypnotized. If so, by following the directions I now give, you can do much toward the end you desire. While you are undressing the child for the night, say, "I shall talk to you tonight while you are asleep and you are to answer me without waking. You will hear and know all mamma says, but you will not wake up." Children as a rule betray great interest in this experiment, and sometimes declare that they will keep awake purposely; but a child's sleep is sound and swift. When the child is fast, asleep you go to her and sit quietly by the bed for a few minutes, stroking her forehead. This will have the effeet of accustoming the sleeper to your presence, and she will be less likely to wake. When you speak, call her by name. Speak low but distinctly. "This is mother talking to you. Sleep quietly. You must not wake. You can speak to me without waking. You are perfectly comfortable and quiet. Sleep sound. Do you hear me talking to you? Say yes. You will not wake up. Now I touch your lips with my fingers, you can speak. Say yes." In many cases it is very difficult at the first attempt to get this answer, but at the second or third it is easily given, generally with a long, drawn-out and hissing sound that makes gravity difficult to sustain. Should the child stir uneasily, and open her eyes you must not relinquish the attempt, but close the eyelids with your fingers and suggest: "Sleeping quietly—nothing will disturb you. You can hear me," etc. Then follow the special suggestion directed to the case in question. They should be forcible, positive suggestions, couched in terms the child can readily understand. Repeat what you say many times slowly. Get the promise if you can.

LESSON NO. 13

Personal magnetism is in possession of every one to a lesser or greater extent. You see it used everywhere. Many were born with this power, others have gained it by long and careful study. To have personal power you must strive to please. Try to forget yourself in making others happy. You must became tactful. In fact, you must have but one object—that to influence. This is very easy when the person to be influenced has been hypnotized by post-hypnotic suggestion. You can make any suggestion you wish, and it will be carried out after the subject has wakened and in apparently his normal condition. You can make suggestions that are not to be carried out or take place for a year if you wish. It is best to hypnotize your subject several times before you make any post-hypnotic suggestion to him, as you must first have caused a deep sleep and gained full control. You can cause post-hypnotic suggestion to take effect immediately after awaking your subjects by commanding them that when they awake they will carry out the suggestion instantly. Be careful and do not give post-hypnotic suggestions that are likely to end unhappily, for remember a subject believes absolutely all you tell him, and you should only give suggestions that are elevating and beneficial, both physically and mentally. By post-hypnotic suggestions you win the undying love or friendship of any subject you may choose. Many people have been united in happy marriages through this wonderful and powerful magnetic influence. You can also by concentration of the will force direct your desires and wishes to others and affect them to a wonderful degree. I have influenced others simply by being in the same room and concentrating my mind on them with the determination of making them follow my will. They never knew that I had influenced them and governed their action. In business this is one of the most powerful agencies.

WILL POWER CAN HYPNOTIZE OTHERS.

METHOD NO. 8.—Is hypnotizing by concentration of the will forces, and is used to hypnotize against the patient's knowledge. It will not succeed in so great a number of cases, still it is often done. You take a comfortable position, and silently, firmly and fixedly regard your subject. You will him or her to sleep by directing your nervous influence upon her, and simply making her the object of your attention. Your subject must be highly sensitive or you will not succeed. After having once been under the influence, a subject is much more easily hypnotized. After you have once hypnotized a person they always become your warm friends.

HOW TO PREVENT ANOTHER FROM GAINING AN INFLENCE OVER YOU, OR HYPNOTIZING YOU.—As soon as you have reason to think some one is trying to hypnotize you for any purpose, place the tips of the fingers of the right hand firmly against the tips of the fingers of the left hand. Hold them this way firmly, and mentally will that you will positively not be influenced. Keep saying, mentally, "I will not be hypnotized by you." Keep your mind continuously on this idea, and you will find that you will become too positive for any one to thoroughly influence or hypnotize you, although you may be made to feel the effects quite plainly by a good hypnotize demonstrator.

LESSON NO. 14

CROSS-HYPNOTISM IS ANOTHER IMPORTANT POINT.—This is caused by more than one person hypnotizing a subject. A subject usually is in communication with only one person at a time, and is therefore perfectly deaf and asleep to all that any one else can do or say. Cross-hypnotism may be caused by others handling, touching, or looking intently at the subject. As soon as the cross-hypnotism occurs the subject will become deaf to your voice, the person that he is crossed with then only has the power to awake him. If the person does not know how to awaken the subject by the former methods given, you must direct him what to do, to awaken the subject, or you can have him talk to the subject, and command him to again go under your control. It may take you some little time to get control, or you may fail to get it altogether. If you do, have the person with whom he is in communication awaken him by the methods given.

You can then put the subject to sleep again and command him to remain under your control, and not go under the control of any other person again without your consent. You can determine who has control of the subject by having each one who has been near him, or touched him, to speak to him and ask him questions. If he does not hear the person and does not answer, he is under the control of some one else, and you should then have each in turn speak to him. You will thereby discover where the control is, and act accordingly. You can put a person in communication with the subject, by having the person take hold of each hand of the subject with each of his. You then command the subject to go under such person's control (naming the person). The subject will immediately become deaf to your voice, but can hear the voice of the one you put him in communication with, while he is utterly deaf to anyone else. I have now given you all the conditions that you are likely to meet with, and by following the method given you are not likely to have any disagreeable experience in your practice of hypnotic experiments.

You can hypnotize two subjects, and in the above manner command them to talk with each other, and also to obey you and they will do as ordered. If you, however, tell them that they are to obey you only, they will do so until you recall it. Always be sure not to give two commands at the same time, as a hypnotized subject can do but one thing at a time.

LESSON NO. 15

CATALEPSY AND ANESTHESIA.—This stage of hypnotism often causes more surprise than any other. Such is the case when the persons present know nothing of this strange science. If physicians are present, or if you have an audience composed of scientific people, this should not be omitted. This will really prove most wonderful and startling to any audience. Hypnotize your subject by any method you wish. Make the passes from his head to his feet, mentally willing that the subject become cataleptic. Put his shoulders on one chair and his feet on another, and have some person stand or sit upon him. The wonderful rigidity of the muscles is a most convincing test in regard to the reality of this strange influence.

Now hypnotize some one who desires a tooth extracted. Make proper suggestions, such as, "You feel no pain. Your face and neck can feel nothing, absolutely nothing." Have a dentist present, and let him extract the tooth. When the subject awakens he will not know his tooth is out. He will suffer no pain whatever—either during or after the operation.

HOW TO HYPNOTIZE WITHOUT PASSES OR TOUCHING YOUR SUBJECT IN ANY WAY.

With some persons it is never well to touch them in any way, as they are annoyed at the familiarity, which will keep you from being successful. This is one of the best methods to use when the subjects are ladies or strangers to you. It is always easy to do this when the subject has once been hypnotized—as with the aid of post-hypnotic suggestion you can produce the sleep by simply saying, "Whenever I snap my fingers, no matter where you are or what you are doing, you are to sleep"—and they will sleep if the subject has really been under your control.

LESSON NO. 16

MY INSTANTANEOUS METHOD of hypnotizing is by giving post-hypnotic suggestion. While the subject is asleep tell him when you point your finger at him, he will become hypnotized instantly, and will come to you at once. He will do so though obstacles almost unsurmountable should be in his way. You have doubtless seen exhibitions where the hypnotist seemed to hypnotize persons back in the audience, the subject coming on the run. This is done by posthypnotic suggestion, and can positively not be done on new subjects.

A PERSON CAN EASILY BE HYPNOTIZED AGAINST HIS WILL, by post-hypnotic suggestion, after having once been controlled. After you get a good control of a subject in private experiments, you can say to him, "At any time in the future I can throw you into the sleep instantly, against your wish, at any time or place." You should say to him, "When I walk up to you and make a pass in front of your face and say, 'sleep,' you will instantly fall asleep." I can hypnotize subjects in the fractional part of a second by this method, and it is the quickest method known to any one. This is a method that has never yet been given to the general public; only a few professionals know it. By practice you will find you can cause some remarkable effects that will not be understood by audiences. They will generally attribute it to your occult power, while to you it will be very plain after you have experimented enough to see the wonderful effects of these suggestions.

HOW TO CONCENTRATE THE WILL.

A good way to train the will so as to concentrate it on one thing is to paste a small piece of white paper, about the size of the end of a lead pencil, in the center of a mirror, seat yourself comfortably and look intently at the paper, trying all the time to keep your mind on the paper and not let it wander. At first your mind will likely wander to other things, but by practice you will get so you can concentrate the will on one thing and keep it there as long as you wish. A hypnotist can hypnotize a good subject just by concentration of the will force after they have learned to concentrate the mind perfectly. To more thoroughly understand, read over my mental method, which is done by the concentrated will—and nothing else.

LESSON NO. 17

When for any reason you want to hypnotize a person who objects, and will not give you the chance to try any method upon him as a last resort, hypnotize him while he sleeps. This of course, is difficult, yet it can be done. Read carefully Lesson No. 12. Apply the same method to induce hypnosis during natural sleep to adults. Such a task could be easily and safely undertaken by the wife or husband. It could be used to cure drunkenness, break bad habits, etc. There is one very important limitation to this method. Hypnotist does not, by his superior will power, compel his patient to abstain from his habits. He merely rouses in him a suggestion which is objectionable to the waking man and will also be objectionable to the sleeping man. All vicious habits and drunkenness are due to mental conditions, but they can be cured by suggestion during sleep, by giving the subject sufficient will power by suggestion when he sleeps. And if the subject wishes to be cured he will be with your aid.

The sleeper must become attentive, or the suggestive treatment in natural sleep is ineffective and useless. The subject must assure you by word of mouth that he is no longer busy with his own fancies, but that his mind is yours. You must be assured that your suggestions are not only heard but understood, realized, become a fact in the sleeper's mind. An easy way to satisfy yourself is, after receiving a response from the lips of the sleeper, take hold of the hand lying nearest you, and raise the arm, saying, "Your arm will stay in the position in which I place it. It will not feel fatigued. It will stay where I put it." Hold the arm in the air for a few seconds, repeating these suggestions, and then let go. If it stays as put, the sleeper's attention is fixed upon you. If it falls there is a condition of weariness present which prevents the suggestion from taking firm hold of the mind, and other suggestions given will be equally ineffective. Therefore, it is well to repeat this experiment, and the suggestions given, until the fixation of the arm in the air attests the fixation of the attention of the sleeper. When this occurs the sleeper has passed into the same mental condition as prevails during induced sleep. He is in relation with you, and will heed and obey your suggestions.

WILL TO SLEEP is nothing more than the mental method, or it can be done by post-hypnotic suggestion.

THE FOLLOWING METHOD is the oldest and for many beginners the best. Seat your subject comfortably in a chair, his back to the light. Tell him to keep his mind from wandering, and to think of nothing but of sleep. Lean his head slightly back, and place your fingers, slightly separated, on his forehead, pressing very lightly. Have him close his eyes and keep them closed, at the same time try and imagine that he can see your fingers as they rest on his forehead about midway between the eyebrows and hair. Tell him to keep his eyes in this position and not let them fall to their natural position, but to keep them trying to see your fingers. Then say in a monotonous but distinct tone, "Your eyelids are getting heavy, heavy, very heavy—heavy. Your eyes are beginning to stick and feel sleepy. You are sleepy; very s-l-e-e-p-y—v-e-r-y s-l-e-e-p-y. Your eyelids can not open. Y-o-u a-r-e a-s-l-e-e-p."

You will now take hold of his right hand with your right hand, and place the ball of your left thumb between the eyebrows of the subject, on the organ of individuality. Allow the fingers to rest on top of the head. Now say to your subject: "You cannot open your eyes, try—try hard." If the subject cannot open his eyes, let loose of his hand and snap your finger and thumb near his left ear, and say, "Now you can open your eyes." If his eyes do not stick you must proceed to hypnotize him deeper, by the foregoing method, doing the work over just as before. Sometimes your Subject will be asleep in four minutes, sometimes a half hour will go by before you succeed, as all persons are not alike, and another method may answer better with same subject; but the larger number of persons will sleep in five or ten minutes.

LESSON NO. 18

HOW TO HYPNOTIZE YOURSELF.—To induce the hypnotic sleep in yourself, seat yourself in an easy rocking chair, with a high back to it. Lean your head back against the back of the chair in an easy position. Relax every muscle in your body and rest in perfect ease. Do not move a muscle. Now close your eyes, directing them inward and downward, at the same time imagining your breath to be a vapor, and mentally watch its inhalation and exhalation through your nostrils. This is termed "transfixion." You will soon begin to feel dizzy, and feel a sinking sensation; in a few minutes you will become utterly powerless to move a muscle, and if you still maintain the concentrated gaze on the imaginary vapor, you will soon pass into the hypnotic sleep, from which you will awake in a short time refreshed both in body and mind.

This method will absolutely cure sleeplessness in any one in a short time. I can go to sleep in less than two minutes any night by this method. I have students who have succeeded at the first and second trials in inducing the hypnotic sleep in themselves. This is a most wonderful fact.

Another good method is to place a small bright object above and twelve inches from your eyes, at an angle of about forty-five degrees. Look at this steadily for a few minutes, while sitting in a comfortable position, with no noise in the room. You will soon get drowsy or have a sinking sensation. When you do so do not resist the inclination to sleep, but let yourself go to sleep in an easy and natural manner. You will sleep from a few minutes to a few hours, and will awake refreshed in body and mind as well. You can also have persons to question you while in this state, and you be enabled to reveal many wonderful and mysterious things regarding the past and future; often you become clairvoyant, as these methods are the ones used to produce clairvoyance by nearly all mediums. It will enable you to foretell future events in your own life as well as incidents in the lives of others. This power can be developed to a wonderful degree if cultivated with a concentration of the whole mind on the subject.

You can cure yourself from pain in the following manner. Rub the part of the body affected for several minutes. Concentrate your mind upon the idea that you have no pain—that it has gone away. Rub the part downward, lightly but briskly. Then press the hand firmly over the suffering part till you feel heat. Repeat to yourself in a low, slow voice, "The pain is leaving—it is gone, the pain has gone entirely away. My limb is warm and comfortable." Then sit down and hypnotize yourself. Let the last thought you have be that you are well, that you are out of pain. When you awaken you will be well. This seldom fails. Never on myself.

LESSON NO. 19

HOW TO HYPNOTIZE A ROOMFUL AT ONE TIME.—This is my method for hypnotizing several persons at a time, and the best one to use on the stage for testing new subjects. After explaining to your volunteers that there is absolutely no danger in being hypnotized by one who fully understands the scientific principles of the art have them take seats. Tell them to place the right hand palm downward over the right knee cap, the left likewise over the left knee cap. Command them to assume as easy a position as possible, allowing every muscle in the body to relax. Slightly incline their heads backward. Command them to close their eyes and look at an imaginary spot exactly in the center of their foreheads, with both eyes, keeping them closed continually. Just at this time let the operator pass around and touch each person directly on the center of the forehead with the end of the forefinger of his right hand, making a slight pressure on the spot touched. Let this be done immediately after the eyes are closed. Command them to hold their eyes absolutely in this position, and not let the eyeballs fall to their normal position. Tell them that it will only be a few seconds until they will feel drowsy and sleepy, and the desire for sleep will take possession of their whole bodies. Absolute quiet and ease of position must be maintained. After allowing them to sit in this position one or two minutes, test them, to secure the sensitive ones for experimenting on. Place your left hand on their right palm downwards, and with your right make a few passes from the center of the forehead down over the eyes, telling them to remain perfectly passive. After making the passes for a minute or more, place your right fingers lightly on top of the head with the fingers slightly parted, press with the ball of your thumb about one inch above the subject's eyes, exactly between them, or in other words, on the organ of "individuality," allowing your left hand in the meantime to rest on the right hand of subject. Tell him that his eyes are now closed fast, and that it will be impossible for him to open them. If he should succeed in opening them, try him once more, the same as before. If he is still refractory, leave him and go on to the next subject, and go through the same process with each. Should his eyes stick and he is unable to open them, snap your fingers near his left ear, and say, "Now you can open them." As soon as he does, command him to "sleep, sleep." Do this two or three times. Now leave him and proceed to do the same with each of your subjects. No matter how hard a subject is to influence, if you persist and he does not resist you will succeed at last. It may take you as much as ten or twenty minutes with new subjects, but after you get them once you will have no more trouble. The first thing to do is to hold the eyes shut, and you need not try any other experiments until you succeed in this. A very important point with a new subject is the confident manner in which you perform the operation, and give the commands and suggestions. Always give them in a firm, low tone of voice. Your will should be concentrated on the sleep of the subjects. Those whose eyes remain closed, let them remain on the stage; send the rest to their seats in the audience. You now begin to make your suggestions to your subjects. By suggestion you can make them laugh, cry, sing, shout, blush or become pale at will.

LESSON NO. 20

HOW TO GIVE AN ENTERTAINMENT.—There is no end to what you can do to make an interesting entertainment. I will give you a few of the things you can do, which will help you in the beginning, but it is well for you to be as original as possible when amusing others.

No. 1.—By suggestion you can lead your subjects into an imaginary garden, where they will behold the beautiful flowers and enjoy the ripe fruit which your suggestions will mentally produce. Some will greedily devour the imaginary fruit, while others will gather the flowers. Some will show selfishness, others will be generous and courteous. Some will enjoy the picturesque, while others will only show the lack of artistic comparison. Some will reveal the spiritual side of their natures, while others will reveal the greed and selfishness of humanity, all corresponding to their own temperament and character.

No. 2.—Mentally you can make one of the subjects discover a swarm of bees in his search for fruit. Suitable suggestions will create in each mind a mental image of bees. The change in these subjects is instantaneous and violent. Some will desperately fight the bees with their hats and hands. Others will roll on the ground, covering their faces and heads to keep from being stung. Some will show anger, others will cry like children, while a few will laugh. You create the bees mentally, then allow each faculty to manifest itself in each subject; no two will be affected alike. All showing the courage or fear of their natures.

No. 3. Put one of your subject's arms in motion. Tell him he cannot stop the movement, and he really cannot.

No. 4. Tell another to walk the floor and he is forced to do so till ordered to stop.

No. 5. Ask another to dance and he dances. All will keep up the motions you wish till you countermand the order.

No. 6. Politely ask a lady subject to sing, and she will sing any song you mentally suggest if she is well under your control.

No. 7. Another subject will play an accompaniment for her, and by suggestion will join in the chorus.

No. 8. You can hand a glass of vinegar to one of your subjects, telling him it is wine, and he will drink all of it, often asking for more.

No. 9. Have a dish of raw vegetables, such as carrots, potatoes, onions, turnips, beets, and any other that you can get. Pass the dish around. Each subject will select something and eat with the same relish as if it were the finest fruit.

No. 10. A small box filled with white beans and dried peas, nicely tied up, can be presented to a lady, with the suggestion that you knew she was fond of candy. She will immediately open the box and pass it to her friends. All will eat and speak of the flavor.

No. 11. Hand a bottle of water to a subject, saying, "it is medicine," and that it is very bitter, but that it will surely cure him. He will take it, making a face, and cough over it when swallowed.

No. 12. Pour a few drops of ammonia on a handkerchief and pass it to a subject with the remark, "this is really a fine and pleasant cologne." The subject will smile and agree with you. While a drop of water passed as ammonia will make the subject sneeze, and tears will start from his eyes.

No. 13. Lay a string across the floor. In an alarmed manner step back from it as you exclaim, "See the water. It is coming this way. We must try to cross it." Some of the subjects will run from it, others will jump over it, others will jump high but fail to cross. People aways laugh at this.

No. 14. You can change the personality of your subjects. Making one or two believe that they are little children. They will laugh and play as if they really were.

No. 15. Then suddenly change them into very old people. Have some deaf, others toothless, others lame, others blind. The transformation from youth to old age will be very funny.

No. 16. Make a young man believe he is a lady. He will

assume a lady's tone and manner. He will laugh and walk like a girl, switching his imaginary skirts about in a very amusing manner.

No. 17. Tie up your handkerchief and tell your subject that it is his little son, and he will care for it with the fondest attention. Tell him it cries and he will attempt to hush it to sleep. Suggest that he is holding a colored baby, and he will throw it down in disgust.

No. 18. Lay down a penny. Tell your subjects that it weighs a ton, and that not one of them can lift it. The effort they all will make is very strange, and often becomes exciting.

No. 19. You can convince your subjects that a cane is a living snake, that a chair is a ferocious animal, or that a pencil is a large reptile.

No. 20. You can make your subjects believe that a cane is a fish-pole, and that a basin of water is a river. A few pieces of paper scattered in the water will add very much to the amusement of the people present. Your subjects will bait their hooks and think that the paper pieces are fish. It is a good plan to tell one that he has a fish on his hook, and that it is so large that he cannot land it. He will use all his force to do so, and tug away at it. Tell another that he has fallen into the river, and that he must swim ashore. The earnestness with which the subjects go through this scene, and their utter astonishment upon being awakened is irresistibly funny.

No. 21. After your subjects have been hypnotized a short time it is a good plan to have them place their hands together (palms against each other). Tell them that they cannot take their hands apart. Have them pull quite hard for a few seconds, straining every nerve and muscle, thoroughly demonstrating to their own satisfaction and to the satisfaction of those present that it is impossible for them to get their hands apart until released from the influence by you. Then you should have them walk stiff-legged. Affect the organ of speech so they cannot say their own names. On this act, make them try hard to speak, as the effect of opening and closing of their mouths very rapidly in the vain effort to utter sound produces a most ludicrous sight. And then this helps in keeping the sleep sound, which is very important. These tests may all be very quickly tried, and they never fail to produce round after round of uproarious laughter. They also inspire those present with confidence in your ability as a hypnotist, and put you in a favorable position for more advanced experiments.

No. 22. Select two or three of your gentlemen subjects, give them each a broom. Tell them, "that they are horses." They will all ride the brooms as if they were, and will give a race at your suggestion.

No. 23. Tell several of your subjects that they belong to an opera company. Have them sing grand opera and comic opera. Also have them sing solos and then make them waltz. As a closing incident to this scene you may have some one dance around the room or the stage with a cane for a partner, telling him that it is a young lady, and that she is the belle of the town.

No. 24. Invite all the hypnotized subjects to take an imaginary balloon ride. Show them various places of interest. Take them to England. Tell them they see London, etc. Then have them visit Paris. Tell them that they can see the prettiest girls in Paris, and have them flirt with them. Tell them that the girls are making faces at them, and that they must make the ugliest faces they can in turn, and not be outdone.

No. 25. Also show them a prize fight between noted prize fighters. Let them see tight rope walkers walking over rivers, etc. Anything that the operator may think of may be introduced. Originate something new and comic. The comments and actions of the subjects in this scene will keep those present in a continuous roar of laughter.

No. 26. If physicians are present, or if you have an audience composed of scientific people, this should not be omitted. It will really prove most wonderful and startling to any audience. Hypnotize your best subject, make all the muscles of the body perfectly rigid. Put his shoulders on one chair and his feet on another, and have several persons stand or sit on him. The wonderful rigidity of the muscles is a most convincing test in regard to the reality of the strange influence.

No. 27. Now make suggestions to one or two of the subjects while they are still asleep. Wake them, and in their natural waking state they will carry out the suggestions, not knowing why, or from whom they received the command.

No. 28. If you have a cigarette smoker present, hypnotize him, make proper suggestions for curing the habit given in Lesson No. 8. Tell him, "that in five minutes after he is awakened he will throw away all the cigarettes he has." Then awaken him, and send him back to his seat. Watch him, and think constantly of what he is to do. When the time is up he will get up, walk towards you, and throw all the cigarettes he has upon the floor.

No. 29. Select a subject who talks easily when under the influence. Hypnotize him and make the suggestion that when he awakens he will be the president of the United States, etc., and that he will make a political speech. Now awaken him, and in a few seconds after he is thoroughly awakened he will get up, a strange look will come into his eyes, and he will commence a remarkable political speech. The power of even the most ignorant person to make a political speech under hypnotic influence is generally most remarkable and baffles explanation.

No. 30. You can hypnotize two or three subjects. Make similar suggestions to them all, and then awaken them all, and they will form a debating society, much to their own surprise.

No. 31. It is well for you to vary these tests under post-hypnotic suggestions. They will prove the most mystifying of the whole evening's entertainment, and will immediately establish your reputation as a hypnotist of extraordinary ability.

No. 32. This is a marvelous scientific test. Show a hypnotized subject a plain white sheet of paper, or a card, make the suggestion that "he is to know that paper, even if it be among a thousand." Have some one mark the sheet very slightly on the back for identification, then mix it with a number of other sheets exactly like it so that no one in his natural condition could possibly pick out the sheet without examining the back of it. Now hand the entire lot of sheets to the hypnotized subject, and he will instantly pick out the sheet first shown him. This test never fails to startle every one present, and it is a most convincing one in regard to the power of hypnotism. You will make converts at every exhibition.

No. 33. Take your hat and go among the spectators and ask several persons to drop any small article into the hat. Do not touch any of them yourself, or let any one do so. After you have obtained ten or twenty different things, give the hat to a hypnotized subject. Tell him to give back each article to the rightful owner. If he should hesitate take his hand and go with him, and after he once starts you will have no trouble. If a good subject is selected he will make no mistake, but give everything back to the right party. That is another wonderful test.

No. 34. Now draw a chalk line across the stage. Place some of the subjects on each side of it, and tell them that they cannot cross it. They will try, but fail.

No. 35. Put a penny on the floor. Tell your subject that it is very heavy, and that he cannot lift it. After he makes several attempts to do so and fails, call another subject to help him. Neither one can lift it till you release the influence.

No. 36. You can make one subject freezing cold, another will fan and pant with the heat.

No. 37. Tell a subject that he is very ill, and he will color and really look and feel ill. Call another and suggest that he cures the sick man. Instantly he will feel his pulse and act the part well.

No. 38. Put a very heavy weight on the floor. Tell your subject "that it is light—nothing to lift." He will raise it easily even if it weighs fifty pounds or more.

No. 39. Lay a number of cards face downward on a table, call up a subject, ask him to tell you what the different cards are. He will do so—not making a single mistake as you will see by lifting each card as he directs.

No. 40. You can make your subjects forget their own names, and imagine that they are some one else.

No. 41. Put a pan of flour on the table and tell a subject to wash his hands. He will think it water and do as you command.

No. 42. You can keep a subject from sitting down, another from getting up. A third will spin round like a top.

No. 43. Place a stick into a subject's hand, suddenly tell him it is a red hot iron. He will drop it with gestures of fear, and blow his breath on his fingers, as if really burnt.

No. 44. Give him a glass with a few drops of water in it; tell him that it is a pint of peanuts, and he will calmly pour them into his pocket.

No. 45. Tell a subject that potatoes are gold pieces, and he will greedily fill his pockets with the bulky vegetables, at the same time express his satisfaction at owning so much money. Then you can tell him he is the richest man in the world.

No. 46. You can make a subject play billiards with a lead pencil for a cue and books for balls.

No. 47. In the midst of doing any of the above, by suggestion you can make the subject become as still as a statue, unable to move. He will stay in any position he was in when you made the command.

No. 48. As a concluding demonstration, a cake walk will be uproariously funny. Get some of the older men, if possible, to allow you to hypnotize them for this experiment, and if you have some peculiar hats put them on the subjects after they are under the influence. As they strut around the room trying the different fancy steps, the spectators will go wild with laughter and enthusiasm. When the subjects are awakened they will not realize they have hats on until they accidentally find it out, and as each one does so his look of utter astonishment will provoke shriek after shriek of laughter.

LESSON NO. 21

MIND READING is a science seldom accomplished by any one in the normal condition or natural state, but when it is two persons must be in perfect rapport with each other, otherwise it would be impossible. There are a few persons who are so highly sensitive that under good conditions they become mind readers. As I understand this wonderful science the reader must be gifted with clairvoyant powers, and by merely touching a person's hand can tell what he is thinking, or can read letters, tell numbers, etc.—provided the second person knows what is to be read. But the most wonderful is the art of mind reading when brought about by hypnotism. Use any method you like best to bring about the sleep. When your subject is under your influence take the third party out of the room. Have him tell you several things for the hypnotized subject to perform. Go back, take the subject's hand, and without speaking, think steadily of the first thing told you that the subject is to do, after a few seconds he will perform the act you mentally have ordered done.

TO GAIN FULL CONTROL OF ANY PERSON YOU MUST FIRST HYPNOTIZE THEM. After you have hypnotized the person you wish to control, and you are very certain they are in a deep sleep, you can give the subject the suggestion that you would have absolute control of him for a certain number of days or hours. You can suggest that he will go where you wish during that length of time.

LESSON NO. 22

TO PUT YOUR SUBJECT INTO A SIX DAY'S TRANCE.—Hypnotize him by any method you wish, or the one that you can induce the deepest sleep with. After he is hypnotized tell him that on a certain day at a certain hour you are going to put him to sleep for one week, that he will have no bad effects from it, but that the sleep will not only benefit but do him much good. Then awaken him. On the said day and time hypnotize him. Be sure you have him in a comfortable position, and that you put him into a deep sleep. Before leaving him, say to him in an earnest way, "You will be sound asleep till I come back. You will be very happy and comfortable till I come back. You will have happy dreams." Make a few passes over him while you are talking. Visit him two or three times a day, each time make the passes over him and always order him to sleep, etc. When you are going to waken him tell him at what hour he is to awaken. For instance, if you want to waken him at four in the afternoon tell him so in the morning when you see him. Never try this long trance unless you are sure of your subject.

When you have subjects that you are very sure of, they can be hypnotized so deeply that teeth can be pulled, also many operations have been performed under this strange influence.

TO HYPNOTIZE ANIMALS.—Some animals can easily be brought into the hypnotic state. Tie the legs of a hen or cock together, hold it down on the ground, the head is pressed down. A chalk line is then drawn on the ground, starting from the bird's beak. The hen will remain motionless. Sparrows, pigeons, rabbits and crabs can be hypnotized the same way.

HYPNOTIZED BY A CARD is done with the aid of suggestion. Tell your subject when he is hypnotized that at any time when you hand him a card he will become instantly hypnotized. Speak in a very forcible manner. If you meet him the next day, or the next week, or month, and offer him a card (no matter where he is, or what he is doing), he will fall at once into the hypnotic condition.

LESSON NO. 23

PERSONAL SUCCESS CAN BE OBTAINED THROUGH HYPNOTISM and the power of suggestion. You will find in matters of business both of great value to you. To illustrate: Supposing two business men come together. One, without the other having the least idea of it, is studying the weak points of his associate. The stronger mind and the most intelligent of the two will eventually bring the other to look upon a subject as he desires, and finally to submit to his wishes. This, then, is suggestion with hypnotic influence, the weaker person is perfectly awake. If you make a point to do so you can make your influence felt upon those about you to such an extent as to advance yourself in many and all ways you wish. Read and study mental method as that is of great assistance where self influence is wanted.

Surgical operations can be performed without a particle of pain by the hypnotist putting the subject to sleep and giving him the suggestion that he will feel nothing. Teeth can be extracted in the same way, as I have proven in numerous cases. You should put the patient to sleep by the method given in any of the former Lessons, then make your suggestions to suit the particular case. After you have your subject completely under the hypnotic influence, and he sits an inert mass before you, speak to him just as though he were awake and in full possession of all his senses. Although asleep to the world he is keenly awake to you. As you have been talking to him and touching him almost constantly he has had no opportunity, to fall asleep on you. Make any suggestion and he will act on it. Give him any command and he will obey. By suggestion after he is awake and apparently all right, yet he is not so in reality, for his volitional power is still withdrawn from the direction you have ordered, so the peremptory command that you gave still exerts its influence over him. Therefore, if you wish to influence him in your favor when he is in the hypnotic sleep, suggest that he shall like you and be willing to obey you. Most subjects become very much attached to you magnetically, and the more you exert your influence the more readily they obey you. You can see examples of the truth of this statement almost daily, when one person seems to have absolute control over another.

LESSON NO. 24

HOW TO MAKE MONEY OUT OF HYPNOTISM is what everyone wants to know. I know that fortunes are being made with the help it gives in many different ways. I will tell you two of the easiest and two of the most successful ways that any one can work up into a money making business, which means much more to you than just a living.

WAY No. 1.—After you are sure you understand hypnotism—understand it so well that you have no trouble whatever in inducing the hypnotic sleep and awaking the subject—you can form classes. (Never have more than ten people in a single class). Hire a good subject and teach your scholars how to hypnotize him. Charge each person $1.00 per lesson. Tell them you can teach them in five lessons how to hypnotize thoroughly and how to awaken their subjects. But never teach but one method for the $5.00. If they want to learn other methods, charge extra for teaching them. You will find that people are willing to pay to learn this science, and will pay much more to learn it from you than by learning through the mails. And it is really worth more. Always make your pupils believe that you are truly a wonderful person. It will pay you to do this.

WAY No. 2.—Perhaps there is as much income in giving entertainments in private houses as there is in classes. But you can do both if you wish. Many charge $25.00 for giving an evening's entertainment which lasts only one hour or so. Some persons who have a very pleasing program get more. It is a good plan to hire one or two good subjects to go with you. Other subjects you will get from among the guests.

LESSON NO. 25

I have now given you full instructions on every necessary point to insure your success, and in this lesson I only want to dwell on what I know to be of the most importance to all beginners. First, never be in a hurry when you want to hypnotize any one. Never doubt your own ability to hypnotize a subject, no matter how long it may take you to gain control. Always be sure your subject breathes slowly and evenly, never in spasms or jerks. Be sure your subject is comfortable in every way before you begin to operate. Never allow any kind of noise in the room, and be careful that your subject has no glare or bright light shining in his face. A moderately lighted room is always best. Be positive that your subject is in a deep sleep before you begin suggestions of any kind. It is always best to make a test of the depth of the sleep before you attempt to perform in any way. An easy and simple test is to say, "You cannot open your eyes," or, "You cannot move your fingers." If the subject is in deep hypnosis, he cannot. If your subject does what you tell him he cannot do, the hypnosis is not deep enough, and you must do the work all over again. When your subject is in a deep sleep he will obey your word and motion. Then and not till then must you begin making suggestions. Never make but one suggestion at a time. Never try to mix up the different methods, for if you do you will fail with them all. Above everything never cross or contradict your subject when he is under the hypnotic influence, as much harm can be done the subject if he is allowed to become excited in any way. Never allow yourself to become excited or annoyed when you have a subject asleep. Do not try to do other things when you have a subject asleep. If you should at any time have a sick subject, and you hypnotize him to give him rest, and want him to sleep several hours, during that time keep as quiet and in as calm a frame of mind yourself as you can—because many subjects are so sensitive that any undue excitement on your part affects them. Your success largely depends on the little things pertaining to hypnotism.

CPSIA information can be obtained at www.ICGtesting.com
Printed in the USA
LVOW10s1318031115

460917LV00001B/13/P

9 781446 506936